Lucy's Home

by Crystal H. Mayo

An Imprint of Mantle Mission Media

Anthony really, really, really, REALLY, really wanted a dog.
DAY after DAY, he would beg his Mama, "Mama, PLEASE, could we have a dog?"

Mama would say,
"Baby, you know that I am NOT a dog person.
Daddy has said NO,
and we DON'T
have room in our home for a dog."

"But Mama..."

Anthony protested.
"I promise to take good care of it.
I would
WALK, FEED, and PLAY
with it all day."

Mama nodded her head,
"Yes, Anthony, I know."

The next day, Mama and Anthony visited PAW-PAW'S house because he had been SICK.

On the way, Anthony asked again. "Mama, are you sure we can't have a DOG?"

Mama took a deep breath and said,
"Baby, you know that I am NOT a dog person.
Daddy has said NO,
and we DON'T
have room in our home for a dog,

BUT..."

Anthony leaned forward in his seat.
Mama looked back and said,
"You can PRAY about it. I don't see how Daddy and
I will ever change our minds, but you can ALWAYS
talk to God about it."

Anthony did. He BOWED his head and whispered a PRAYER to God.

Meanwhile, across town, a rambunctious LITTLE dog loved BIG adventures.

She would often wiggle her way OUT from under the fence and RUN as FAST as her short legs would carry her.

She would often try to RUN faster than the CARS on the street.

On the way to Paw-Paw's house, Anthony spotted her on the road and yelled, "MAMA, A DOG!"

This dog was running without a care in the world. She was darting between cars on a busy street.

People were honking their horns, trying to get her to move off the road.

Mama quickly pulled into Paw-Paw's driveway and called for the DOG to come over safely.

Paw-Paw came outside to SEE what all the commotion was about.

Anthony tried to catch her, but this cute little dog ran FAST, like lightning, right past him and into Paw-Paw's house.

Once inside, the DOG grabbed Paw-Paw's white SOCKS and tossed them into the air to PLAY.

Paw-Paw wanted his socks back, but she wouldn't LET them GO.
Paw-Paw played tug-of-war with her.

Everyone laughed at how SILLY she was.

Anthony asked, "Mama, can we KEEP her?"

Mama said,
"Baby, you know that I am NOT a dog person,
Daddy has said NO,
and we DON'T
have room in our home for a dog."

"She is NOT ours to keep.
We need to FIND her home."
Anthony hoped that it could be HIS home.

Anthony and his mama went from HOUSE to HOUSE, asking the neighbors if they knew this ADORABLE dog.

Most did not, but one neighbor thought she came from the blue house at the end of the street. They went to that blue house and KNOCKED on the door, but no one came.

They returned to Paw-Paw's house and bathed the dog. She loved taking a BATH as Mama scrubbed her clean.

When Mama took her out of the bath, she ran down the hallway, shaking off the WATER and rolling around on the FLOOR.

Paw-Paw thought she was a CUTE dog and said he would like a dog just like her.

MAMA explained that they could not find the dog's owner.

Paw-Paw understood and offered to KEEP her in the meantime. He said, "I'm going to call her LUCY."

Every day they would go to Paw-Paw's house to visit.

The whole family would play fetch, chase, and tug-of-war with LUCY.

They would take her on long WALKS.

She loved to SIT in the SUN and watch for squirrel to chase under the shady tree.

Mama would cook healthy FOOD for Paw-Paw, but it wasn't his favorite. So, when Mama was not looking, he would give the food to LUCY instead.

She loved the YUMMY treats and sat by his side faithfully every day. Paw-Paw petted LUCY and was thankful for her being such a GOOD dog and a loving companion.

There came a day when Paw-Paw couldn't care
for LUCY anymore, and she needed
a new HOME.

Mama took Lucy to the veterinarian to see if she
was registered with anyone, but they said NO.

Returning to the neighborhood, Mama noticed a MAN standing outside the blue house. Could this be Lucy's HOME?

She stopped and asked, "Hi, sir. Could you tell me if you know this dog?"

"Yes", he said. "I recognize her, but I DON'T remember her name." He said she had been his dog but could not keep her anymore. He told Mama to FIND her a good home.

Mama decided to take Lucy HOME in the meantime.

Anthony believed that God answered his prayers. He picked up Lucy and showed her around his HOME.

His sister was so excited to have another girl in the house that she dressed Lucy up, painted her NAILS, and put hair BOWS all over her.

Daddy taught Lucy some tricks.
She learned how to
SIT, SHAKE, LIE DOWN, ROLL OVER,
and even how to DANCE.

Lucy taught Daddy some tricks, too.
She could SING!

One day, his brother was playing Paw-Paw's ACCORDION, and she burst out in song.

The day finally came when
Lucy got a home where she belonged.

Even though Mama was
NOT a dog person,
Daddy said NO,
and they did NOT have room in their
home for a dog...

Because Mama BECAME a dog person,
Daddy said YES,
and they ALL made room
in their HOME and hearts for LUCY.

Reading comprehension questions for Lucy's Home

1. Who did Mama and Anthony go visit?
   - a.   Maw-Maw
   - b.   A friend
   - c.   Paw-Paw
   - d.   Daddy
2. Why did Mama tell Anthony to pray about getting a dog?
   - a.   They already had a pet dog at home.
   - b.   Neither Mama nor Daddy wanted a dog.
   - c.   They didn't have a fence around the backyard.
   - d.   Sister is allergic to dogs.
3. What made Mama pull the car over so quickly?
   - a.   A squirrel darted in the street.
   - b.   A little boy fell off his bicycle.
   - c.   A dog was running in the road without a care in the world.
   - d.   Paw-Paw was outside in the front yard.
4. What did Paw-Paw give Lucy?
   - a.   A collar to wear around her neck.
   - b.   A bone to chew on.
   - c.   The healthy food Mama cooked for Paw-Paw
   - d.   A doghouse.
5. How did Anthony know that God answered his prayer for a dog?
   - a.   Mama became a dog person.
   - b.   Daddy said Yes.
   - c.   They all made room in their home and in their hearts for Lucy.
   - d.   All of the above.

Dear Reader,

Do you believe God hears our prayers? I hope our true story shows that He does! God blessed our family with Lucy in a way we never expected, and it all started with one small prayer.

I can't promise that you will get a dog if you pray. But I can promise this—God knows what is best. Sometimes He says yes, sometimes no, and sometimes the answer is steady and slow. Every time, His answer is good, and we can trust that His love never fails.

So keep praying—just like Anthony did.

With love,

Crystal H. Mayo

"Now to him who is able to do immeasurably more than all we ask or imagine, according to his power that is at work within us to him be glory...in Christ Jesus throughout all generations, for ever and ever! Amen." ~ Ephesians 3:20-21 (NIV)

MORE LUCY

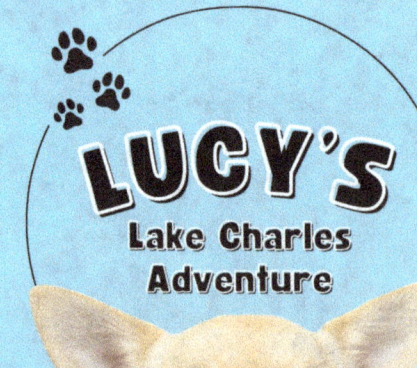

 **FREE DOWNLOADS**

An Imprint of Mantle Mission Media

"In those days when you pray, I will listen. If you look for Me wholeheartedly, you will find Me." ~ Jeremiah 29:12-13 (NLT)

Special thanks to:
- God, for answering Anthony's prayer with Lucy.
- Doug, for saying yes and giving her a loving home.
- Buddy, Sandy, Molly, Victor, David, Megan, Erin, and Jeff for helping bring Lucy's Home to life.

Dedicated to my children:

May you always keep that child-like faith and remember that God hears, sees, and knows those wishes we keep deep inside. May He give you the desires of your heart as you dream big and do it all for His Glory!

I love you so much ~Mama.

LUCY'S HOME

Copyright © 2023 by Crystal H. Mayo
Watercolor illustrations were AI generated by Crystal H. Mayo using Canva and MidJourney.
Papics Photography by Megan Stevens
Author Headshot by Christina Custodio
Reading Comprehension Questions by Karen Ashworth

All rights reserved. No part of this publication may be reproduced, distributed, or transmitted in any form or by any means, electronic or mechanical, including photocopying, recording, or by an information and storage retrieval system, without prior written consent from the copyright holder.

Scripture quotations marked NIV are taken from the Holy Bible, New International Version (R), NIV (R), Copyright © 1973, 1978, 1984, 2011 by Biblica, Inc. (R). Used with permission. All rights reserved worldwide.

Scripture quotations marked NLT are taken from the Holy Bible, New Living Translation, copyright © 1996, 2004, 2015, by Tyndale House Foundation. Used by permission of Tyndall House Publishers, Inc., Carol Stream, Illinois 60188. All rights reserved.

Library of Congress Cataloging-in-Publication Data
Library of Congress Control Number: 2023921915

ISBN: 979-8-9894969-0-7 (Paperback)
ISBN: 979-8-9894969-3-8 (HC)

First edition 2023
Hardcover edition 2025

All inquiries should be directed to:
Crystal H. Mayo
crystal@crystalhmayo.com
www.crystalhmayo.com

An Imprint of Mantle Mission Media

www.ingramcontent.com/pod-product-compliance
Lightning Source LLC
Chambersburg PA
CBHW081356130526
44581CB00013B/109